# About This Book

**Title:** *Star Patterns*

**Step:** 6

**Word Count:** 276

**Skills in Focus:** All vowel-r combinations

**Tricky Words:** constellation, telescopes, because, Orion, centaur

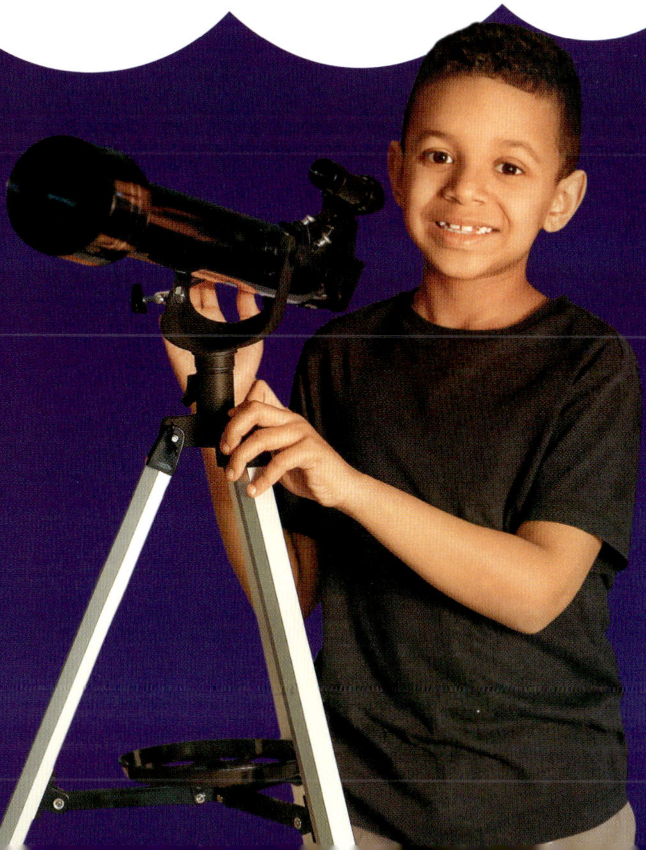

# Ideas for Using This Book

## Before Reading:

- **Comprehension:** Look at the title and cover image together. Walk through the pictures in the book with readers and have them make predictions about what they might learn while reading.
- **Accuracy:** Practice saying the tricky words listed on page 1.
- **Phonics:** Tell students they will read words with the vowel-r combinations *ar*, *er*, *ir*, *or*, and *ur*. Write each letter combination on a piece of paper in a five-column format. Look at the word *star* in the title on the front cover. Ask readers to point to the vowel-r combination that says /ar/. Write this word under the *ar* column, underlining the letters that represent *r* and the vowel that comes before it. Repeat with the story words *pattern*, *orbits*, *burn*, and *girl*. Have readers look through the first few pages of the book to see if they can find any other words with vowel-r combinations (ex: *orbs*, *glitter*, *hard*). Does the *r* change how the vowel before it is pronounced?

## During Reading:

- Have readers point under each word as they read it.
- **Decoding:** If readers are stuck on a word, help them say each sound and blend the sounds together smoothly. Point out words with vowel-r combinations as they appear.
- **Comprehension:** Invite students to talk about what new things they are learning about stars while reading. What are they learning that they didn't know before?

## After Reading:

Discuss the book. Some ideas for questions:

- Have you ever looked for constellations in the night sky? Which constellations have you seen before?
- What do you still wonder about stars?

# Star Patterns

Text by Laura Stickney

Reading Consultant
Deborah MacPhee, PhD
Professor, School of Teaching and Learning
Illinois State University

PICTURE WINDOW BOOKS
a capstone imprint

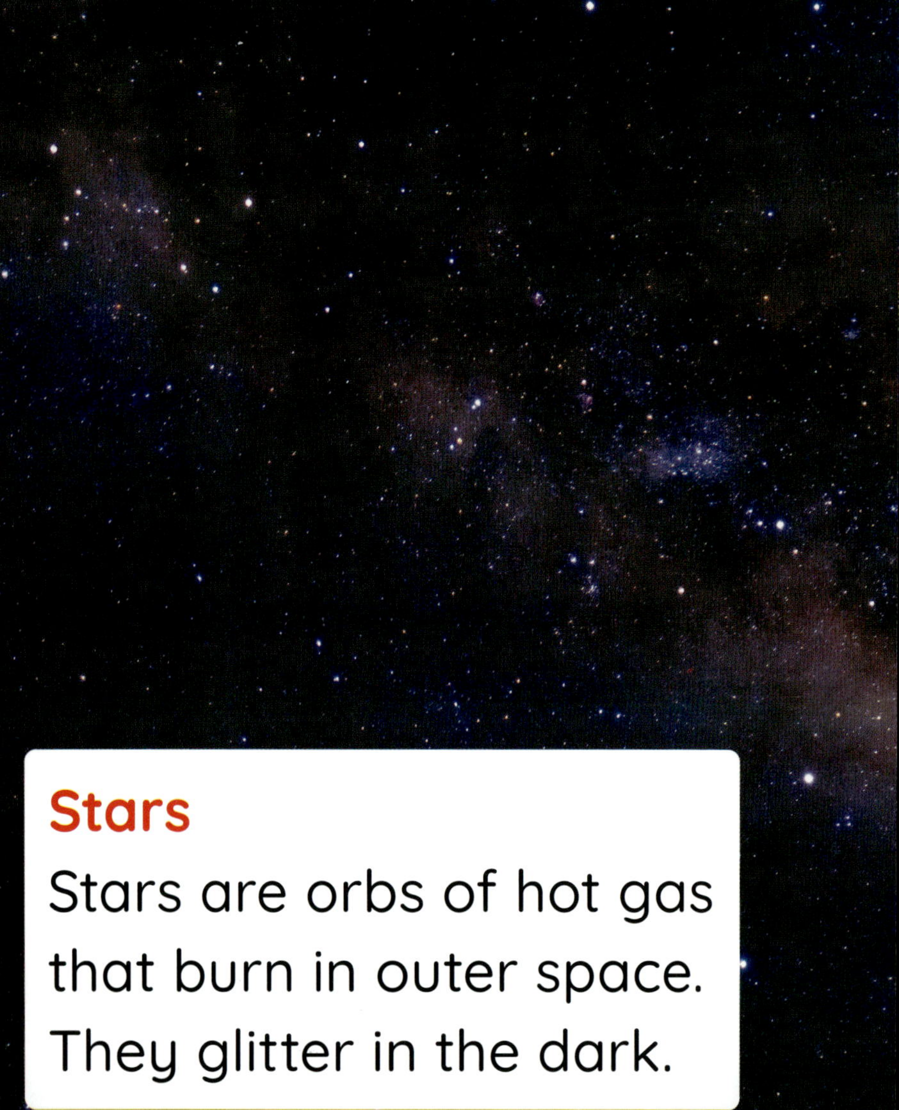

## Stars

Stars are orbs of hot gas that burn in outer space. They glitter in the dark.

At night, you can see stars in the sky from Earth. But you can't see stars during the day.

It can also be hard to see stars when clouds cover them.

Some stars form patterns called constellations.

People made up these patterns.

They connected the dots of stars in the sky to form shapes.

Many constellations form the shapes of critters or people from stories.

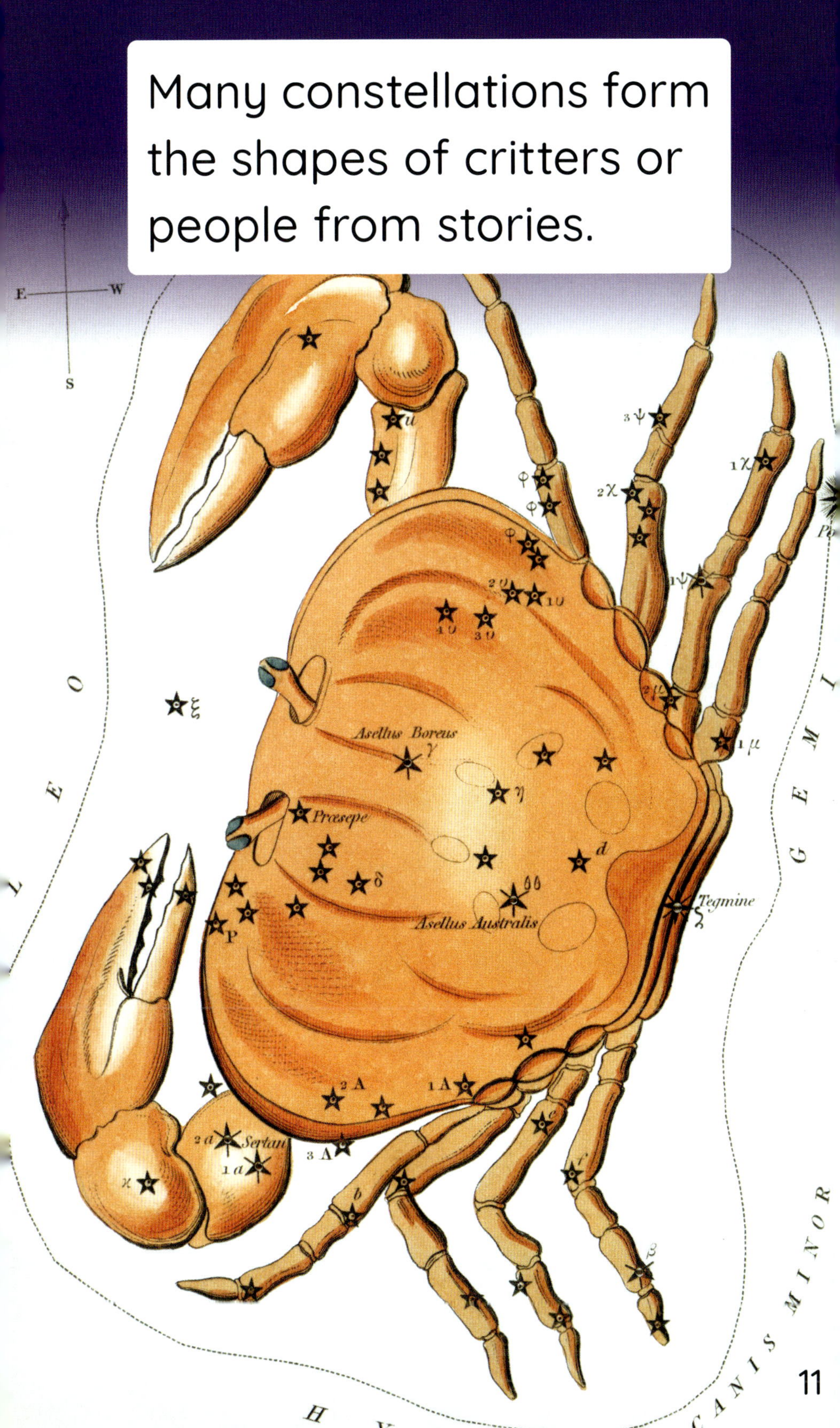

You can use telescopes to stargaze, or observe stars. Telescopes make things far away look bigger.

You can set up telescopes in yards or parks.

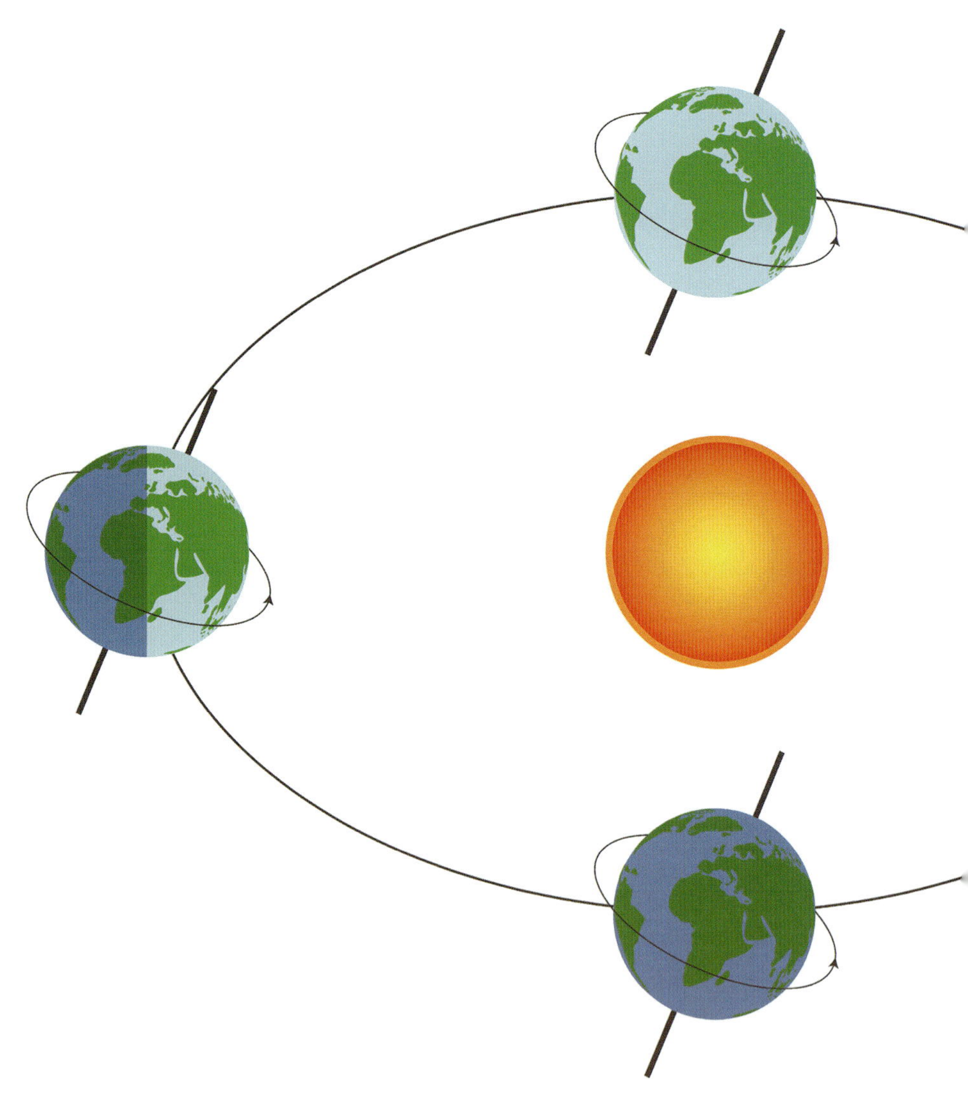

## The Changing Sky

You can see different star patterns at different times of the year.

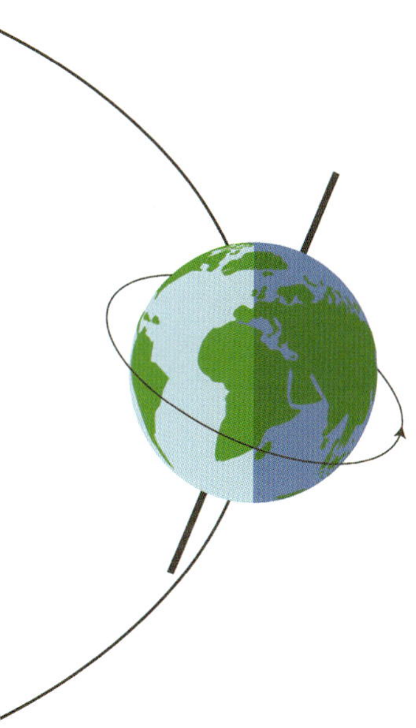

This is because Earth orbits around the sun in space.

As Earth orbits, we see different parts of the sky.

People in the north or south may see different star patterns.

Some constellations are easier to see in certain seasons.

Others are seen year-round.

Spotting Star Patterns
The Big Dipper and Little Dipper can be seen all year in the North.

The North Star is part of the Little Dipper. People can use it to find their way north.

In winter, nights are longer. It is easier to observe stars.

Orion the hunter is one constellation seen during winter.

Virgo is easier to see in spring. It is shaped like a girl.

Summer has warmer weather but shorter nights. This makes stargazing harder.

Beach-Hut

In summer, look for a scorpion constellation. Its name is Scorpius.

Look for Centaurus. It is a centaur. It has a man's torso and a horse's body.

Let's observe the stars!

# More Ideas:

## Phonics Activity

### Playing Memory with Vowel-r Words:

Prepare two sets of cards (using two different colors) to play a game of Memory. On one set of cards, write the vowel-r words from the story. For each word, prepare a separate card with the corresponding vowel-r combination (in a different color). Place the cards face down on a surface. Have students take turns turning two cards over, one of each color. To make a match, students must read the word on the card and have the matching letter combination. Continue playing until all cards have been matched.

Suggested words:

**ar**: star, dark, hard, yards, parks, far, parts

**er**: patterns, outer, critters, certain, dipper, weather

**ir**: Virgo, girl

**or**: orbs, form, stories, orbits, north, torso

**ur**: during, burn

## Extended Learning Activity

### Stargazing:

Have readers go outside at night and observe the sky. Ask them to think about what star patterns they notice. Can they find any constellations? Then have readers write a few sentences about their observations. Challenge readers to use vowel-r words in their sentences.

Published by Picture Window Books, an imprint of Capstone
1710 Roe Crest Drive, North Mankato, Minnesota 56003
capstonepub.com



Library of Congress Cataloging-in-Publication Data is available on the Library of Congress website.

ISBN: 9798875277948 (hardback)
ISBN: 9798875277900 (paperback)
ISBN: 9798875277887 (eBook PDF)

Image Credits: Getty: Imgorthand, 16–17, RichVintage, 26–27, standret, 2–3, stevecoleimages, front cover; Shutterstock: Al Calvillo, 18–19, 32, Allexxandar, 24–25, Angela Cini, 14–15, AstroStar, 13, back cover, delcarmat, 29, Favious, 7, johannweitweg, 22–23, New Africa, 6, Pike-28, 8–9, Pixel-Shot, 1, 12, 30, Rawpixel.com, 10, 11, Savvapanf Photo, 20–21, sripfoto, 4–5, 28

Printed and bound in China. PO 6460